This book belongs to:

_____

How to use this Prayer Journal

This is a 60-day prayer journal and can be utilized to explore God's word surrounding different aspects of your life.

How to enjoy the book, Step by Step:

- You will find a list of subjects and corresponding Bible verses on the next page (page 3).

- Each day, select a verse.

- Place a check mark in the circle next to the verse you select indicating that you have completed your studies of the verse

- You will find a space at the top of each day's page to write in the verse that you selected for that day.

- Follow the prompts provided.

STRESS

- ○ Psalm 46:1-3
- ○ Philippians 4:6
- ○ John 14:27
- ○ Psalm 94:19
- ○ Luke 12:25-26
- ○ John 14:27
- ○ Joshua 1:9

FEAR

- ○ Luke 12:22-26
- ○ Psalm 55:22
- ○ Deuteronomy 31:6
- ○ Psalm 46:1
- ○ Psalm 118:6-7
- ○ Psalm 34:4
- ○ Psalm 56:3

HEALTH

- ○ Proverbs 17:22
- ○ Jeremiah 33:6
- ○ Proverbs 16:24
- ○ Proverbs 3:7-8
- ○ Jeremiah 17:14
- ○ Exodus 23:25
- ○ Isaiah 41:10

STRENGTH

- ○ Philippians 4:13
- ○ Isaiah 40:29
- ○ Psalm 119:28
- ○ Ephesians 6:10
- ○ Isaiah 40:31
- ○ Psalm 46:1
- ○ Isaiah 41:10

FAITH

- ○ Hebrews 11:1
- ○ Matthew 21:22
- ○ Romans 10:17
- ○ Mark 11:22-24
- ○ 1 Corinthians 2:5
- ○ Luke 1:37
- ○ 2 Corinthians 5:7

STRUGGLES

- ○ Isaiah 41:13
- ○ 1 Peter 5:7
- ○ James 1:2-4
- ○ Proverbs 3:5-6
- ○ Proverbs 12:25
- ○ Romans 8:28
- ○ James 1:12

PROTECTION

- ○ Psalm 138:7
- ○ Deuteronomy 31:6
- ○ Psalm 20:1
- ○ Psalm 34:19
- ○ Psalm 51:1
- ○ Psalm 140:4

HOPE

- ○ Hebrews 11:11
- ○ Isaiah 40:31
- ○ Jeremiah 29:11
- ○ Romans 5:5
- ○ Romans 15:13
- ○ Romans 8:24-25

BE THANKFUL

- ○ 1 Chronicles 16:34
- ○ Colossians 3:17
- ○ Colossians 4:2
- ○ Philippians 4:6
- ○ Psalm 28:7
- ○ Psalm 106:1

Today's Date:_____

Let God speak to you through his Word. Select a scripture from Page 3.

Scripture selected:_____

Write down the scripture:

Study the scripture, then pray and answer the following.

Write down how you're feeling about the topic of the scripture:

_____

_____

_____

_____

What's your prayer to God surrounding the scripture?

_____

_____

_____

_____

Other Prayer Requests:

_____ _____

_____ _____

_____ _____

_____ _____

Answered Prayer Requests:

_____ _____

_____ _____

_____ _____

_____ _____

Today I am most thankful for:

_____

_____

_____

_____

Today's Date:_____

Let God speak to you through his Word. Select a scripture from Page 3.

Scripture selected:_____

Write down the scripture:

Study the scripture, then pray and answer the following.

Write down how you're feeling about the topic of the scripture:

_____

_____

_____

_____

What's your prayer to God surrounding the scripture?

_____

_____

_____

_____

Other Prayer Requests:

_____   _____

_____   _____

_____   _____

_____   _____

Answered Prayer Requests:

_____   _____

_____   _____

_____   _____

_____   _____

Today I am most thankful for:

_____

_____

_____

_____

Today's Date:_____

Let God speak to you through his Word. Select a scripture from Page 3.

Scripture selected:_____

Write down the scripture:

Study the scripture, then pray and answer the following.

Write down how you're feeling about the topic of the scripture:

_____

_____

_____

_____

What's your prayer to God surrounding the scripture?

_____

_____

_____

_____

Other Prayer Requests:

_____   _____

_____   _____

_____   _____

_____   _____

Answered Prayer Requests:

_____   _____

_____   _____

_____   _____

_____   _____

Today I am most thankful for:

_____

_____

_____

_____

Today's Date:_____

Let God speak to you through his Word. Select a scripture from Page 3.

Scripture selected:_____

Write down the scripture:

Study the scripture, then pray and answer the following.

Write down how you're feeling about the topic of the scripture:

_____

_____

_____

_____

What's your prayer to God surrounding the scripture?

_____

_____

_____

_____

Other Prayer Requests:

_____ _____

_____ _____

_____ _____

_____ _____

Answered Prayer Requests:

_____ _____

_____ _____

_____ _____

_____ _____

Today I am most thankful for:

_____

_____

_____

_____

Today's Date:_____

Let God speak to you through his Word. Select a scripture from Page 3.

Scripture selected:_____

Write down the scripture:

Study the scripture, then pray and answer the following.

Write down how you're feeling about the topic of the scripture:

_____

_____

_____

_____

What's your prayer to God surrounding the scripture?

_____

_____

_____

_____

Other Prayer Requests:

_____   _____

_____   _____

_____   _____

_____   _____

Answered Prayer Requests:

_____   _____

_____   _____

_____   _____

_____   _____

Today I am most thankful for:

_____

_____

_____

_____

Today's Date:_____

Let God speak to you through his Word. Select a scripture from Page 3.

Scripture selected:_____

Write down the scripture:

Study the scripture, then pray and answer the following.

Write down how you're feeling about the topic of the scripture:

_____

_____

_____

_____

What's your prayer to God surrounding the scripture?

_____

_____

_____

_____

Other Prayer Requests:

_____   _____

_____   _____

_____   _____

_____   _____

Answered Prayer Requests:

_____   _____

_____   _____

_____   _____

_____   _____

Today I am most thankful for:

_____

_____

_____

_____

Today's Date:_____

Let God speak to you through his Word. Select a scripture from Page 3.

Scripture selected:_____

Write down the scripture:

Study the scripture, then pray and answer the following.

Write down how you're feeling about the topic of the scripture:

_____

_____

_____

_____

What's your prayer to God surrounding the scripture?

_____

_____

_____

_____

Other Prayer Requests:

_____   _____

_____   _____

_____   _____

_____   _____

Answered Prayer Requests:

_____   _____

_____   _____

_____   _____

_____   _____

Today I am most thankful for:

_____

_____

_____

_____

Today's Date:_____

Let God speak to you through his Word. Select a scripture from Page 3.

Scripture selected:_____

Write down the scripture:

Study the scripture, then pray and answer the following.

Write down how you're feeling about the topic of the scripture:

_____

_____

_____

_____

What's your prayer to God surrounding the scripture?

_____

_____

_____

_____

Other Prayer Requests:

_____   _____

_____   _____

_____   _____

_____   _____

Answered Prayer Requests:

_____   _____

_____   _____

_____   _____

_____   _____

Today I am most thankful for:

_____

_____

_____

_____

Today's Date:_____

Let God speak to you through his Word. Select a scripture from Page 3.

Scripture selected:_____

Write down the scripture:

Study the scripture, then pray and answer the following.

Write down how you're feeling about the topic of the scripture:

_____

_____

_____

_____

What's your prayer to God surrounding the scripture?

_____

_____

_____

_____

Other Prayer Requests:

_____   _____

_____   _____

_____   _____

_____   _____

Answered Prayer Requests:

_____   _____

_____   _____

_____   _____

_____   _____

Today I am most thankful for:

_____

_____

_____

_____

Today's Date:_____

Let God speak to you through his Word. Select a scripture from Page 3.

Scripture selected:_____

Write down the scripture:

Study the scripture, then pray and answer the following.

Write down how you're feeling about the topic of the scripture:

_____

_____

_____

_____

What's your prayer to God surrounding the scripture?

_____

_____

_____

_____

Other Prayer Requests:

_____ _____

_____ _____

_____ _____

_____ _____

Answered Prayer Requests:

_____ _____

_____ _____

_____ _____

_____ _____

Today I am most thankful for:

_____

_____

_____

_____

Today's Date:_____

Let God speak to you through his word. Select a scripture from Page 3.

Scripture selected:_____

Write down the scripture:

Study the scripture, then pray and answer the following.

Write down how you're feeling about the topic of the scripture:

_____

_____

_____

_____

What's your prayer to God surrounding the scripture?

_____

_____

_____

_____

Other Prayer Requests:

_____   _____

_____   _____

_____   _____

_____   _____

Answered Prayer Requests:

_____   _____

_____   _____

_____   _____

_____   _____

Today I am most thankful for:

_____

_____

_____

_____

Today's Date:_____

Let God speak to you through his Word. Select a scripture from Page 3.

Scripture selected:_____

Write down the scripture:

Study the scripture, then pray and answer the following.

Write down how you're feeling about the topic of the scripture:

_____

_____

_____

_____

What's your prayer to God surrounding the scripture?

_____

_____

_____

_____

Other Prayer Requests:

_____   _____

_____   _____

_____   _____

_____   _____

Answered Prayer Requests:

_____   _____

_____   _____

_____   _____

_____   _____

Today I am most thankful for:

_____

_____

_____

_____

Today's Date:_____

Let God speak to you through his Word. Select a scripture from Page 3.

Scripture selected:_____

Write down the scripture:

Study the scripture, then pray and answer the following.

Write down how you're feeling about the topic of the scripture:

_____

_____

_____

_____

What's your prayer to God surrounding the scripture?

_____

_____

_____

_____

Other Prayer Requests:

_____   _____

_____   _____

_____   _____

_____   _____

Answered Prayer Requests:

_____   _____

_____   _____

_____   _____

_____   _____

Today I am most thankful for:

_____

_____

_____

_____

Today's Date:_____

Let God speak to you through his Word. Select a scripture from Page 3.

Scripture selected:_____

Write down the scripture:

Study the scripture, then pray and answer the following.

Write down how you're feeling about the topic of the scripture:

_____

_____

_____

_____

What's your prayer to God surrounding the scripture?

_____

_____

_____

_____

Other Prayer Requests:

_____   _____

_____   _____

_____   _____

_____   _____

Answered Prayer Requests:

_____   _____

_____   _____

_____   _____

_____   _____

Today I am most thankful for:

_____

_____

_____

_____

Today's Date:_____

Let God speak to you through his Word. Select a scripture from Page 3.

Scripture selected:_____

Write down the scripture:

Study the scripture, then pray and answer the following.

Write down how you're feeling about the topic of the scripture:

_____

_____

_____

_____

What's your prayer to God surrounding the scripture?

_____

_____

_____

_____

Other Prayer Requests:

_____   _____

_____   _____

_____   _____

_____   _____

Answered Prayer Requests:

_____   _____

_____   _____

_____   _____

_____   _____

Today I am most thankful for:

_____

_____

_____

_____

Today's Date:_____

Let God speak to you through his Word. Select a scripture from Page 3.

Scripture selected:_____

Write down the scripture:

Study the scripture, then pray and answer the following.

Write down how you're feeling about the topic of the scripture:

_____

_____

_____

_____

What's your prayer to God surrounding the scripture?

_____

_____

_____

_____

Other Prayer Requests:

_____ _____

_____ _____

_____ _____

_____ _____

Answered Prayer Requests:

_____ _____

_____ _____

_____ _____

_____ _____

Today I am most thankful for:

_____

_____

_____

_____

Today's Date:_____

Let God speak to you through his Word. Select a scripture from Page 3.

Scripture selected:_____

Write down the scripture:

Study the scripture, then pray and answer the following.

Write down how you're feeling about the topic of the scripture:

_____

_____

_____

_____

What's your prayer to God surrounding the scripture?

_____

_____

_____

_____

Other Prayer Requests:

_____   _____

_____   _____

_____   _____

_____   _____

Answered Prayer Requests:

_____   _____

_____   _____

_____   _____

_____   _____

Today I am most thankful for:

_____

_____

_____

_____

Today's Date:_____

Let God speak to you through his Word. Select a scripture from Page 3.

Scripture selected:_____

Write down the scripture:

Study the scripture, then pray and answer the following.

Write down how you're feeling about the topic of the scripture:

_____

_____

_____

_____

What's your prayer to God surrounding the scripture?

_____

_____

_____

_____

Other Prayer Requests:

_____   _____

_____   _____

_____   _____

_____   _____

Answered Prayer Requests:

_____   _____

_____   _____

_____   _____

_____   _____

Today I am most thankful for:

_____

_____

_____

_____

Today's Date:_____

Let God speak to you through his Word. Select a scripture from Page 3.

Scripture selected:_____

Write down the scripture:

Study the scripture, then pray and answer the following.

Write down how you're feeling about the topic of the scripture:

_____

_____

_____

_____

What's your prayer to God surrounding the scripture?

_____

_____

_____

_____

Other Prayer Requests:

_____   _____

_____   _____

_____   _____

_____   _____

Answered Prayer Requests:

_____   _____

_____   _____

_____   _____

_____   _____

Today I am most thankful for:

_____

_____

_____

_____

Today's Date:_____

Let God speak to you through his Word. Select a scripture from Page 3.

Scripture selected:_____

Write down the scripture:

Study the scripture, then pray and answer the following.

Write down how you're feeling about the topic of the scripture:

_____

_____

_____

_____

What's your prayer to God surrounding the scripture?

_____

_____

_____

_____

Other Prayer Requests:

_____   _____

_____   _____

_____   _____

_____   _____

Answered Prayer Requests:

_____   _____

_____   _____

_____   _____

_____   _____

Today I am most thankful for:

_____

_____

_____

_____

Today's Date:_____

Let God speak to you through his Word. Select a scripture from Page 3.

Scripture selected:_____

Write down the scripture:

Study the scripture, then pray and answer the following.

Write down how you're feeling about the topic of the scripture:

_____

_____

_____

_____

What's your prayer to God surrounding the scripture?

_____

_____

_____

_____

Other Prayer Requests:

_____   _____

_____   _____

_____   _____

_____   _____

Answered Prayer Requests:

_____   _____

_____   _____

_____   _____

_____   _____

Today I am most thankful for:

_____

_____

_____

_____

Today's Date:_____

Let God speak to you through his Word. Select a scripture from Page 3.

Scripture selected:_____

Write down the scripture:

Study the scripture, then pray and answer the following.

Write down how you're feeling about the topic of the scripture:

_____

_____

_____

_____

What's your prayer to God surrounding the scripture?

_____

_____

_____

_____

Other Prayer Requests:

_____   _____

_____   _____

_____   _____

_____   _____

Answered Prayer Requests:

_____   _____

_____   _____

_____   _____

_____   _____

Today I am most thankful for:

_____

_____

_____

_____

Today's Date:_____

Let God speak to you through his Word. Select a scripture from Page 3.

Scripture selected:_____

Write down the scripture:

Study the scripture, then pray and answer the following.

Write down how you're feeling about the topic of the scripture:

_____

_____

_____

_____

What's your prayer to God surrounding the scripture?

_____

_____

_____

_____

Other Prayer Requests:

_____   _____

_____   _____

_____   _____

_____   _____

Answered Prayer Requests:

_____   _____

_____   _____

_____   _____

_____   _____

Today I am most thankful for:

_____

_____

_____

_____

Today's Date:_____

Let God speak to you through his Word. Select a scripture from Page 3.

Scripture selected:_____

Write down the scripture:

Study the scripture, then pray and answer the following.

Write down how you're feeling about the topic of the scripture:

_____

_____

_____

_____

What's your prayer to God surrounding the scripture?

_____

_____

_____

_____

Other Prayer Requests:

_____   _____

_____   _____

_____   _____

_____   _____

Answered Prayer Requests:

_____   _____

_____   _____

_____   _____

_____   _____

Today I am most thankful for:

_____

_____

_____

_____

Today's Date:_____

Let God speak to you through his Word. Select a scripture from Page 3.

Scripture selected:_____

Write down the scripture:

Study the scripture, then pray and answer the following.

Write down how you're feeling about the topic of the scripture:

_____

_____

_____

_____

What's your prayer to God surrounding the scripture?

_____

_____

_____

_____

Other Prayer Requests:

_____   _____

_____   _____

_____   _____

_____   _____

Answered Prayer Requests:

_____   _____

_____   _____

_____   _____

_____   _____

Today I am most thankful for:

_____

_____

_____

_____

Today's Date:_____

Let God speak to you through his Word. Select a scripture from Page 3.

Scripture selected:_____

Write down the scripture:

Study the scripture, then pray and answer the following.

Write down how you're feeling about the topic of the scripture:

_____

_____

_____

_____

What's your prayer to God surrounding the scripture?

_____

_____

_____

_____

Other Prayer Requests:

_____   _____

_____   _____

_____   _____

_____   _____

Answered Prayer Requests:

_____   _____

_____   _____

_____   _____

_____   _____

Today I am most thankful for:

_____

_____

_____

_____

Today's Date:_____

Let God speak to you through his Word. Select a scripture from Page 3.

Scripture selected:_____

Write down the scripture:

Study the scripture, then pray and answer the following.

Write down how you're feeling about the topic of the scripture:

_____

_____

_____

_____

What's your prayer to God surrounding the scripture?

_____

_____

_____

_____

Other Prayer Requests:

_____   _____

_____   _____

_____   _____

_____   _____

Answered Prayer Requests:

_____   _____

_____   _____

_____   _____

_____   _____

Today I am most thankful for:

_____

_____

_____

_____

Today's Date:_____

Let God speak to you through his Word. Select a scripture from Page 3.

Scripture selected:_____

Write down the scripture:

Study the scripture, then pray and answer the following.

Write down how you're feeling about the topic of the scripture:

_____

_____

_____

_____

What's your prayer to God surrounding the scripture?

_____

_____

_____

_____

Other Prayer Requests:

_____ _____

_____ _____

_____ _____

_____ _____

Answered Prayer Requests:

_____ _____

_____ _____

_____ _____

_____ _____

Today I am most thankful for:

_____

_____

_____

_____

Today's Date:_____

Let God speak to you through his Word. Select a scripture from Page 3.

Scripture selected:_____

Write down the scripture:

Study the scripture, then pray and answer the following.

⟳⟲·⟳⟲·⟳⟲·⟳⟲·⟳⟲·⟳⟲·

Write down how you're feeling about the topic of the scripture:

_____

_____

_____

_____

⟳⟲·⟳⟲·⟳⟲·⟳⟲·⟳⟲·⟳⟲·

What's your prayer to God surrounding the scripture?

_____

_____

_____

_____

Other Prayer Requests:

_____   _____

_____   _____

_____   _____

_____   _____

Answered Prayer Requests:

_____   _____

_____   _____

_____   _____

_____   _____

Today I am most thankful for:

_____

_____

_____

_____

Today's Date:_____

Let God speak to you through his Word. Select a scripture from Page 3.

Scripture selected:_____

Write down the scripture:

Study the scripture, then pray and answer the following.

Write down how you're feeling about the topic of the scripture:

_____

_____

_____

_____

What's your prayer to God surrounding the scripture?

_____

_____

_____

_____

Other Prayer Requests:

_____   _____

_____   _____

_____   _____

_____   _____

Answered Prayer Requests:

_____   _____

_____   _____

_____   _____

_____   _____

Today I am most thankful for:

_____

_____

_____

_____

Today's Date:_____

Let God speak to you through his Word. Select a scripture from Page 3.

Scripture selected:_____

Write down the scripture:

Study the scripture, then pray and answer the following.

Write down how you're feeling about the topic of the scripture:

_____

_____

_____

_____

What's your prayer to God surrounding the scripture?

_____

_____

_____

_____

Other Prayer Requests:

_____   _____

_____   _____

_____   _____

_____   _____

Answered Prayer Requests:

_____   _____

_____   _____

_____   _____

_____   _____

Today I am most thankful for:

_____

_____

_____

_____

Today's Date:_____

Let God speak to you through his Word. Select a scripture from Page 3.

Scripture selected:_____

Write down the scripture:

Study the scripture, then pray and answer the following.

Write down how you're feeling about the topic of the scripture:

_____

_____

_____

_____

What's your prayer to God surrounding the scripture?

_____

_____

_____

_____

Other Prayer Requests:

_____   _____

_____   _____

_____   _____

_____   _____

Answered Prayer Requests:

_____   _____

_____   _____

_____   _____

_____   _____

Today I am most thankful for:

_____

_____

_____

_____

Today's Date:_____

Let God speak to you through his Word. Select a scripture from Page 3.

Scripture selected:_____

Write down the scripture:

Study the scripture, then pray and answer the following.

Write down how you're feeling about the topic of the scripture:

_____

_____

_____

_____

What's your prayer to God surrounding the scripture?

_____

_____

_____

_____

Other Prayer Requests:

_____   _____

_____   _____

_____   _____

_____   _____

Answered Prayer Requests:

_____   _____

_____   _____

_____   _____

_____   _____

Today I am most thankful for:

_____

_____

_____

_____

Today's Date:_____

Let God speak to you through his Word. Select a scripture from Page 3.

Scripture selected:_____

Write down the scripture:

Study the scripture, then pray and answer the following.

Write down how you're feeling about the topic of the scripture:

_____

_____

_____

_____

What's your prayer to God surrounding the scripture?

_____

_____

_____

_____

Other Prayer Requests:

_____   _____

_____   _____

_____   _____

_____   _____

Answered Prayer Requests:

_____   _____

_____   _____

_____   _____

_____   _____

Today I am most thankful for:

_____

_____

_____

_____

Today's Date:_____

Let God speak to you through his Word. Select a scripture from Page 3.

Scripture selected:_____

Write down the scripture:

Study the scripture, then pray and answer the following.

Write down how you're feeling about the topic of the scripture:

_____

_____

_____

_____

What's your prayer to God surrounding the scripture?

_____

_____

_____

_____

Other Prayer Requests:

_____   _____

_____   _____

_____   _____

_____   _____

Answered Prayer Requests:

_____   _____

_____   _____

_____   _____

_____   _____

Today I am most thankful for:

_____

_____

_____

_____

Today's Date:_____

Let God speak to you through his Word. Select a scripture from Page 3.

Scripture selected:_____

Write down the scripture:

Study the scripture, then pray and answer the following.

Write down how you're feeling about the topic of the scripture:

_____

_____

_____

_____

What's your prayer to God surrounding the scripture?

_____

_____

_____

_____

Other Prayer Requests:

_____   _____

_____   _____

_____   _____

_____   _____

Answered Prayer Requests:

_____   _____

_____   _____

_____   _____

_____   _____

Today I am most thankful for:

_____

_____

_____

_____

Today's Date:_____

Let God speak to you through his Word. Select a scripture from Page 3.

Scripture selected:_____

Write down the scripture:

Study the scripture, then pray and answer the following.

Write down how you're feeling about the topic of the scripture:

_____

_____

_____

_____

What's your prayer to God surrounding the scripture?

_____

_____

_____

_____

Other Prayer Requests:

_____   _____

_____   _____

_____   _____

_____   _____

Answered Prayer Requests:

_____   _____

_____   _____

_____   _____

_____   _____

Today I am most thankful for:

_____

_____

_____

_____

Today's Date:_____

Let God speak to you through his Word. Select a scripture from Page 3.

Scripture selected:_____

Write down the scripture:

Study the scripture, then pray and answer the following.

Write down how you're feeling about the topic of the scripture:

_____

_____

_____

_____

What's your prayer to God surrounding the scripture?

_____

_____

_____

_____

Other Prayer Requests:

_____   _____

_____   _____

_____   _____

_____   _____

Answered Prayer Requests:

_____   _____

_____   _____

_____   _____

_____   _____

Today I am most thankful for:

_____

_____

_____

_____

Today's Date:_____

Let God speak to you through his Word. Select a scripture from Page 3.

Scripture selected:_____

Write down the scripture:

Study the scripture, then pray and answer the following.

Write down how you're feeling about the topic of the scripture:

_____

_____

_____

_____

What's your prayer to God surrounding the scripture?

_____

_____

_____

_____

Other Prayer Requests:

_____   _____

_____   _____

_____   _____

_____   _____

Answered Prayer Requests:

_____   _____

_____   _____

_____   _____

_____   _____

Today I am most thankful for:

_____

_____

_____

_____

Today's Date:_____

Let God speak to you through his Word. Select a scripture from Page 3.

Scripture selected:_____

Write down the scripture:

Study the scripture, then pray and answer the following.

Write down how you're feeling about the topic of the scripture:

_____

_____

_____

_____

What's your prayer to God surrounding the scripture?

_____

_____

_____

_____

Other Prayer Requests:

_____   _____

_____   _____

_____   _____

_____   _____

Answered Prayer Requests:

_____   _____

_____   _____

_____   _____

_____   _____

Today I am most thankful for:

_____

_____

_____

_____

Today's Date:_____

Let God speak to you through his Word. Select a scripture from Page 3.

Scripture selected:_____

Write down the scripture:

Study the scripture, then pray and answer the following.

Write down how you're feeling about the topic of the scripture:

_____

_____

_____

_____

What's your prayer to God surrounding the scripture?

_____

_____

_____

_____

Other Prayer Requests:

_____   _____

_____   _____

_____   _____

_____   _____

Answered Prayer Requests:

_____   _____

_____   _____

_____   _____

_____   _____

Today I am most thankful for:

_____

_____

_____

_____

Today's Date:_____

Let God speak to you through his Word. Select a scripture from Page 3.

Scripture selected:_____

Write down the scripture:

Study the scripture, then pray and answer the following.

Write down how you're feeling about the topic of the scripture:

_____

_____

_____

_____

What's your prayer to God surrounding the scripture?

_____

_____

_____

_____

Other Prayer Requests:

_____   _____

_____   _____

_____   _____

_____   _____

Answered Prayer Requests:

_____   _____

_____   _____

_____   _____

_____   _____

Today I am most thankful for:

_____

_____

_____

_____

Today's Date:_____

Let God speak to you through his Word. Select a scripture from Page 3.

Scripture selected:_____

Write down the scripture:

Study the scripture, then pray and answer the following.

Write down how you're feeling about the topic of the scripture:

_____

_____

_____

_____

What's your prayer to God surrounding the scripture?

_____

_____

_____

_____

Other Prayer Requests:

_____   _____

_____   _____

_____   _____

_____   _____

Answered Prayer Requests:

_____   _____

_____   _____

_____   _____

_____   _____

Today I am most thankful for:

_____

_____

_____

_____

Today's Date:_____

Let God speak to you through his Word. Select a scripture from Page 3.

Scripture selected:_____

Write down the scripture:

Study the scripture, then pray and answer the following.

Write down how you're feeling about the topic of the scripture:

_____

_____

_____

_____

What's your prayer to God surrounding the scripture?

_____

_____

_____

_____

Other Prayer Requests:

_____ _____

_____ _____

_____ _____

_____ _____

Answered Prayer Requests:

_____ _____

_____ _____

_____ _____

_____ _____

Today I am most thankful for:

_____

_____

_____

_____

Today's Date:_____

Let God speak to you through his Word. Select a scripture from Page 3.

Scripture selected:_____

Write down the scripture:

Study the scripture, then pray and answer the following.

Write down how you're feeling about the topic of the scripture:

_____

_____

_____

_____

What's your prayer to God surrounding the scripture?

_____

_____

_____

_____

Other Prayer Requests:

_____ _____

_____ _____

_____ _____

_____ _____

Answered Prayer Requests:

_____ _____

_____ _____

_____ _____

_____ _____

Today I am most thankful for:

_____

_____

_____

_____

Today's Date:_____

Let God speak to you through his Word. Select a scripture from Page 3.

Scripture selected:_____

Write down the scripture:

Study the scripture, then pray and answer the following.

Write down how you're feeling about the topic of the scripture:

_____

_____

_____

_____

What's your prayer to God surrounding the scripture?

_____

_____

_____

_____

Other Prayer Requests:

_____ _____

_____ _____

_____ _____

_____ _____

Answered Prayer Requests:

_____ _____

_____ _____

_____ _____

_____ _____

Today I am most thankful for:

_____

_____

_____

_____

Today's Date:_____

Let God speak to you through his Word. Select a scripture from Page 3.

Scripture selected:_____

Write down the scripture:

Study the scripture, then pray and answer the following.

Write down how you're feeling about the topic of the scripture:

_____

_____

_____

_____

What's your prayer to God surrounding the scripture?

_____

_____

_____

_____

Other Prayer Requests:

_____   _____

_____   _____

_____   _____

_____   _____

Answered Prayer Requests:

_____   _____

_____   _____

_____   _____

_____   _____

Today I am most thankful for:

_____

_____

_____

_____

Today's Date:_____

Let God speak to you through his Word. Select a scripture from Page 3.

Scripture selected:_____

Write down the scripture:

Study the scripture, then pray and answer the following.

Write down how you're feeling about the topic of the scripture:

_____

_____

_____

_____

What's your prayer to God surrounding the scripture?

_____

_____

_____

_____

Other Prayer Requests:

_____   _____

_____   _____

_____   _____

_____   _____

Answered Prayer Requests:

_____   _____

_____   _____

_____   _____

_____   _____

Today I am most thankful for:

_____

_____

_____

_____

Today's Date:_____

Let God speak to you through his Word. Select a scripture from Page 3.

Scripture selected:_____

Write down the scripture:

Study the scripture, then pray and answer the following.

Write down how you're feeling about the topic of the scripture:

_____

_____

_____

_____

What's your prayer to God surrounding the scripture?

_____

_____

_____

_____

Other Prayer Requests:

_____   _____

_____   _____

_____   _____

_____   _____

Answered Prayer Requests:

_____   _____

_____   _____

_____   _____

_____   _____

Today I am most thankful for:

_____

_____

_____

_____

Today's Date:_____

Let God speak to you through his Word. Select a scripture from Page 3.

Scripture selected:_____

Write down the scripture:

Study the scripture, then pray and answer the following.

Write down how you're feeling about the topic of the scripture:

_____

_____

_____

_____

What's your prayer to God surrounding the scripture?

_____

_____

_____

_____

Other Prayer Requests:

_____   _____

_____   _____

_____   _____

_____   _____

Answered Prayer Requests:

_____   _____

_____   _____

_____   _____

_____   _____

Today I am most thankful for:

_____

_____

_____

_____

Today's Date:_____

Let God speak to you through his Word. Select a scripture from Page 3.

Scripture selected:_____

Write down the scripture:

Study the scripture, then pray and answer the following.

Write down how you're feeling about the topic of the scripture:

_____

_____

_____

_____

What's your prayer to God surrounding the scripture?

_____

_____

_____

_____

Other Prayer Requests:

_____   _____

_____   _____

_____   _____

_____   _____

Answered Prayer Requests:

_____   _____

_____   _____

_____   _____

_____   _____

Today I am most thankful for:

_____

_____

_____

_____

Today's Date:_____

Let God speak to you through his Word. Select a scripture from Page 3.

Scripture selected:_____

Write down the scripture:

Study the scripture, then pray and answer the following.

Write down how you're feeling about the topic of the scripture:

_____

_____

_____

_____

What's your prayer to God surrounding the scripture?

_____

_____

_____

_____

Other Prayer Requests:

_____   _____

_____   _____

_____   _____

_____   _____

Answered Prayer Requests:

_____   _____

_____   _____

_____   _____

_____   _____

Today I am most thankful for:

_____

_____

_____

_____

Today's Date:_____

Let God speak to you through his Word. Select a scripture from Page 3.

Scripture selected:_____

Write down the scripture:

Study the scripture, then pray and answer the following.

Write down how you're feeling about the topic of the scripture:

_____

_____

_____

_____

What's your prayer to God surrounding the scripture?

_____

_____

_____

_____

Other Prayer Requests:

_____   _____

_____   _____

_____   _____

_____   _____

Answered Prayer Requests:

_____   _____

_____   _____

_____   _____

_____   _____

Today I am most thankful for:

_____

_____

_____

_____

Today's Date:_____

Let God speak to you through his Word. Select a scripture from Page 3.

Scripture selected:_____

Write down the scripture:

Study the scripture, then pray and answer the following.

Write down how you're feeling about the topic of the scripture:

_____

_____

_____

_____

What's your prayer to God surrounding the scripture?

_____

_____

_____

_____

Other Prayer Requests:

_____   _____

_____   _____

_____   _____

_____   _____

Answered Prayer Requests:

_____   _____

_____   _____

_____   _____

_____   _____

Today I am most thankful for:

_____

_____

_____

_____

Today's Date:_____

Let God speak to you through his Word. Select a scripture from Page 3.

Scripture selected:_____

Write down the scripture:

Study the scripture, then pray and answer the following.

Write down how you're feeling about the topic of the scripture:

_____

_____

_____

_____

What's your prayer to God surrounding the scripture?

_____

_____

_____

_____

Other Prayer Requests:

_____   _____

_____   _____

_____   _____

_____   _____

Answered Prayer Requests:

_____   _____

_____   _____

_____   _____

_____   _____

Today I am most thankful for:

_____

_____

_____

_____

Today's Date:_____

Let God speak to you through his Word. Select a scripture from Page 3.

Scripture selected:_____

Write down the scripture:

Study the scripture, then pray and answer the following.

~~~~~~~~~~~~~~~~~~~~~~~~~~~~~~~~~~~~~

Write down how you're feeling about the topic of the scripture:

_____

_____

_____

_____

~~~~~~~~~~~~~~~~~~~~~~~~~~~~~~~~~~~~~

What's your prayer to God surrounding the scripture?

_____

_____

_____

_____

Other Prayer Requests:

_____ _____

_____ _____

_____ _____

_____ _____

Answered Prayer Requests:

_____ _____

_____ _____

_____ _____

_____ _____

Today I am most thankful for:

_____

_____

_____

_____

Today's Date:_____

Let God speak to you through his Word. Select a scripture from Page 3.

Scripture selected:_____

Write down the scripture:

Study the scripture, then pray and answer the following.

Write down how you're feeling about the topic of the scripture:

_____

_____

_____

_____

What's your prayer to God surrounding the scripture?

_____

_____

_____

_____

Other Prayer Requests:

_____   _____

_____   _____

_____   _____

_____   _____

Answered Prayer Requests:

_____   _____

_____   _____

_____   _____

_____   _____

Today I am most thankful for:

_____

_____

_____

_____

Today's Date:_____

Let God speak to you through his Word. Select a scripture from Page 3.

Scripture selected:_____

Write down the scripture:

Study the scripture, then pray and answer the following.

Write down how you're feeling about the topic of the scripture:

_____

_____

_____

_____

What's your prayer to God surrounding the scripture?

_____

_____

_____

_____

Other Prayer Requests:

_____   _____

_____   _____

_____   _____

_____   _____

Answered Prayer Requests:

_____   _____

_____   _____

_____   _____

_____   _____

Today I am most thankful for:

_____

_____

_____

_____

Today's Date:_____

Let God speak to you through his Word. Select a scripture from Page 3.

Scripture selected:_____

Write down the scripture:

Study the scripture, then pray and answer the following.

Write down how you're feeling about the topic of the scripture:

_____

_____

_____

_____

What's your prayer to God surrounding the scripture?

_____

_____

_____

_____

Other Prayer Requests:

_____   _____

_____   _____

_____   _____

_____   _____

Answered Prayer Requests:

_____   _____

_____   _____

_____   _____

_____   _____

Today I am most thankful for:

_____

_____

_____

_____

Today's Date:_____

Let God speak to you through his Word. Select a scripture from Page 3.

Scripture selected:_____

Write down the scripture:

Study the scripture, then pray and answer the following.

Write down how you're feeling about the topic of the scripture:

_____

_____

_____

_____

What's your prayer to God surrounding the scripture?

_____

_____

_____

_____

Other Prayer Requests:

_____   _____

_____   _____

_____   _____

_____   _____

Answered Prayer Requests:

_____   _____

_____   _____

_____   _____

_____   _____

Today I am most thankful for:

_____

_____

_____

_____

Made in the USA
Monee, IL
08 March 2024

54645007R00070